Jazz AND VISUAL IMPROVISATIONS

CATHERINE BERNARD GUEST CURATOR
STANLEY CROUCH CONTRIBUTING ESSAYIST

MAJOR FUNDING FOR THIS EXHIBITION WAS PROVIDED BY AT&T. ADDITIONAL SUPPORT HAS BEEN PROVIDED BY THE WESTCHESTER
ARTS COUNCIL, WHICH IS SUPPORTED BY WESTCHESTER COUNTY, CORPORATIONS, FOUNDATIONS, AND INDIVIDUALS; AND THE EXHIBITION PATRONS
OF THE KATONAH MUSEUM OF ART. THE CATALOGUE IS FUNDED IN PART BY A GRANT FROM THE IDA AND WILLIAM ROSENTHAL FOUNDATION.

acknowledgments FOR THE PAST TEN SUMMERS, THE KATONAH Museum of Art has held a series of jazz concerts in the sculpture garden. The range of music categorized as jazz and the various ways jazz standards are interpreted testify to the complexity of this American art form. Realizing that an exhibition dealing with jazz would be equally compelling, the Exhibitions Committee was delighted when Catherine Bernard, Assistant Professor of Art History at SUNY Old Westbury, proposed *Jazz and Visual Improvisations*. We are grateful to Ms. Bernard for her determined efforts to secure the best works of art available to support her thesis and for accepting with grace the occasional disappointment. She wrote an intelligent and well-researched essay on the role of improvisation in the visual arts. We appreciate her leading us to Stanley Crouch, whose additional contribution on the American origins of jazz enhances the catalogue. As amiable colleagues, they both added to the pleasure of working on this project.

A special thanks must go to the lenders and the artists participating in the exhibition. And we join Ms. Bernard in acknowledging the contributions made by Ani Boyajian, Editor, Stuart Davis Catalogue Raisonné; Leslie Brenner; Earl Davis; Annie Gawlak, Fine Art Consultant; Helen Harrison, Director, Pollock-Krasner House and Study Center; Zach Miner, Gagosian Gallery; Thierry Pérémarti, journalist for the French magazine *Jazzman*; Miya Rakotoarivony-Sanson, Merton Simpson Gallery; and Spencer Richards.

A team of Museum volunteers and staff worked with characteristic dedication to assure the highest standards for *Jazz and Visual Improvisations*. Nancy Wallach, Director of Exhibitions, and her Co-Project Director for this exhibition, Fran Alexander, attended to every aspect of its implementation with finesse and imagination. Yvonne Pollack, Docent Trainer, and Ezra Shales, Director of Education, provided insightful interpretations and educational programs. Aline Benjamin and Nancy Wallach edited the catalogue, which was thoughtfully designed by Edvin Yegir. Michael Prudhom, who designed the exhibition, also supervised its installation. Anne Holman, the Registrar, carefully attended to myriad details. We thank them all.

Jazz and Visual Improvisations was funded in part by a generous grant from AT&T. For his support for the Katonah Museum of Art, his faith in this project, and his dedication to the arts in Westchester County, we are indebted to Robin Flowers, Regional Vice-President – Public Relations for AT&T.

Jazz and Visual Improvisations THROUGHOUT THE
twentieth century, jazz has been a powerful cultural force. Improvisation, inarguably the core of jazz, has allowed the musician to perpetually reinvent the music in a constantly evolving form that has kept it alive for almost a hundred years. In the visual arts also, improvisation has had a significant impact on the development of original art forms and aesthetic systems.[1]

Jazz and Visual Improvisations looks at jazz and creative improvisation as quintessential forces in the development of American art after World War II. Since improvisation is open-ended, it allows for constant development and transformation. It is the historical importance of this particular transforming aspect that *Jazz and Visual Improvisations* proposes to explore. Jazz has mirrored decisive episodes of American history and politics and continues today to play a defining role in our culture *because* of its improvised nature.

JAZZ, IMPROVISATION, AND AMERICAN MODERNISM AFTER WORLD WAR II
In the late 1940s, as the New York School of Abstract Expressionism was emerging, jazz was also undergoing significant changes of style and structure. After World War II the big bands were overshadowed by smaller bands, quartets or quintets, which brought to the development of jazz music a greater flexibility and attention to individual expression. Improvised solos, an important part of the swing bands, became even more prominently featured in the bebop era that followed. With the insistence on improvised solo sequences in post-war jazz music, a more introspective style of creativity emerged, one that spawned heroic figures. Pioneer soloists such as Charlie Parker in music and Jackson Pollock in painting have often been compared because of their relentless search for originality. Bebop became a quintessential urban music, just as the New York School came to symbolize American urban culture in the eyes of the art world.

The emergence of existentialism, which took on a specific form on this side of the Atlantic, played a major part in the development of this new introspective creativity. To the fateful nihilism that characterized French existentialism, American artists responded in a characteristic manner with pragmatism; existentialism here became intertwined with action. In the visual arts it was expressed as action painting, where the artist defined himself or herself through the gesture, leaving a concrete mark on the surface of the canvas. In jazz music, it can be argued that it revolved around the growth of the experimental solo. In both cases, it should also be noted, the audience was asked to redefine itself and to become more introspective – to listen rather than dance, or to reflect upon the new abstract language rather than read a figure-oriented narrative.

The daily music of gesture painters almost without exception was jazz, particularly Bop, so much that the famous jazz club, the Five Spot Cafe (whose walls were covered with announcements of artists' shows) was sustained initially by an artist clientele.[2]

The importance of jazz in the creation of a new aesthetic was recognized by the artistic community of the time. In 1946, the Kootz Gallery in New York organized an exhibition entitled *Homage to Jazz* with works by Gottlieb, Baziotes, Motherwell, Bearden, Holty, and Browne.[3] In this post-war context, jazz was a crucial cultural force in the development of American Modernism. With improvisation as an essential aspect of the creative process – a practice also quickly absorbed by visual artists of the New York School and writers of the Beat Generation[4] – jazz musicians established a vernacular art form.

IMPROVISATION AND VISUAL LANGUAGE

One of the foremost pioneers of American Modernism is Stuart Davis. Davis always asserted that abstract elements of color and form were the real subject matter of painting. He developed a discrete pictorial system onto which he superimposed social and cultural discourses. The importance of jazz in the development of this system is undeniable. Jazz remained a constant influence throughout Davis's career, and he considered it an essential component of American culture.

Jazz has been a continuous source of inspiration in my work from the very beginning for the simple reason that I regard it as the one American art which seems to me to have the same quality of art that I found in the best modern European painting.[5]

The inspiration that Davis drew from jazz goes beyond subject matter. He also borrowed from it a structural model, based on the interrelationship of instruments playing together, which he transformed into the simultaneous sequencing of the painting's surface. Davis listened intently to the music of pianist Earl Hines. Romare Bearden, then a young artist, visited Davis often around 1940 and remembered his advice: "Listen to what he isn't playing. What you don't need is just as important as what you do need."[6] Once Bearden asked Davis why he liked Hines so much, and Davis answered: "For his wonderful sense of intervals."[7] The intervals and the space in Hines's music find a counterpart in Davis's placement of colors and shapes and in the rhythmic juxtaposition of the diverse pictorial elements.

Davis's *Pad No. 4* [PLATE 7] is part of a series of paintings executed between 1945 and 1951. The word "PAD" appears in each work in the series, as a theme around which the series is constructed, similar to theme variations in jazz. The composition of *Pad No. 4* is a complex arrangement of letters and squiggles that hover above different color planes in much the same way as a solo or an improvised phrase relates to the rhythmic structure in a jazz composition. The visual association to jazz is confirmed by the manner in which Davis worked:

Tell your friend that I have always liked hot music. There's something wrong with any American who doesn't. But I never realized that it was influencing my work until one day I put on a favorite record and listened to it while I was looking at a painting I had just finished. Then I got a funny feeling. If I looked, or if I listened, there was no shifting of attention. It seemed to amount to the same thing – like twins, a kinship. After that, for a long time, I played records while I painted.[8]

This parallel between jazz and visual language may also be applied to the work of Frank Bowling, an artist who came of age with post-war abstraction. When he arrived in New York in 1963, Bowling went regularly to the Five Spot Cafe to listen to the music that he had previously known in his native Guyana only from records. The two paintings in the exhibition, *ornettescornet* [PLATE 6] and *aboutmidnightlastnight*, pay homage to Ornette Coleman and Thelonious Monk. The color combinations in each painting reflect the sensibility of their music. Bowling also listens to jazz when he paints:

I work on the floor and the wall. During this time, I am not very conscious of my surroundings. And all of a sudden something will come on, like Ornette blowing something, and I become acutely aware that I am going along with it. Him and me, we are doing the music and the painting all together.[9]

Sophisticated variations and color harmonies are fundamental aspects of Charles Seliger's work. Seliger acknowledges jazz as a major creative force that he visually translates into a complex exploration of organic forms, endlessly reworked, like subtle variations on a theme, refining colors and shapes. The jewel-like surfaces of *Nearer the Stars* [PLATE 16] also recall ancient Persian miniatures, another source for his painting. The intricacy of harmonies, the complexity of arrangements, and the subtle variations encountered in the music of Charlie Haden and Lenny Tristano, two of his favorite jazz musicians, are echoed here as well.

Larry Rivers began his career as a jazz musician. Although by the late 1940s his involvement with jazz as a performer had decreased dramatically, jazz remains to this day an important source of his creative energy. Often referred to as gestural realism, Larry Rivers's work is difficult to categorize since it underwent many drastic changes throughout his career. There is, however, a common thread: he constantly mixes and matches references drawn from old masters, pop culture, and history. A definition given to his friend O'Hara's poetry – a "smorgasbord of the recognizable"[10] – can be applied to his own work; it characterizes his particular strategy of mixing and improvising.

In 1958, Rivers worked towards a more unified approach to the canvas, simplifying the images and organizing the surfaces with homogeneous color fields. In *The Drummer* [PLATE 15] the movements of the musician and the beats on the drum are recorded by the rapid brushwork and a liquid texture that evoke the speed of the rhythm and the fluidity of the musical experience. Rivers combines a painterly approach with his intimate knowledge of jazz.

The creation of an improvised language based upon jazz is fundamental to the art of Romare Bearden, who grew up in the 1920s and 1930s during the Harlem Renaissance. Bearden's parents were prominent social and civic figures in Harlem; friends of the family included Fats Waller and Duke Ellington, who became Bearden's first collectors.

Bearden started to work with collage in 1963, at a time when he and other African-American artists, including Norman Lewis and Merton Simpson, founded a group called Spiral to further the recognition of black artists in America. As a collaborative work, Bearden suggested making a collage about black life using magazine photos. He went on to develop this technique, creating several series: *The Prevalence of Rituals*, 1972-73; *Of the Blues*, 1974; *Odysseus*, 1977; *Mecklenburg County*, 1978-79; and *Jazz*, 1980. Working in thematic series is comparable to the way jazz musicians improvise from standard songs; in both cases a theme is repeated and then improvised upon.

In Bearden's collages, an improvised aesthetic is evidenced in the compositions, the color associations, and the cut-out technique. The colors establish changing rhythms. In *Soul Three*, for example, the hot pinks and oranges are balanced by cool blues and greens to create a counterpoint. A similar rhythmic variation is created in *Uptown Sunday Night Session* [COVER], where the white circular shapes are offset by the red spots. The angular forms in *Improvisations* [PLATE 5] relate to the variations in tempo, harmonies, and melody that are also characteristic of jazz improvisation. The intersecting surfaces and jagged shapes in these collages create surprise effects, and the diversity of the materials used help to underline the improvised nature of the process. Bearden explained: "I paint out of the tradition of the blues, of call and recall. You start a theme and you call and recall."[11]

"Call and recall," a prominent feature of African-American music, can be traced back to the tradition of work songs and further to West African music. "Call and recall" similarly defines a visual system, present in some popular art forms of the southern United States; for example, in African-American quilts it translates as variations on a theme, repetition, and changes in patterns and color contrasts. These elements combine to form an aesthetic present in both music and the visual arts.

IMPROVISATION AND THE SEARCH FOR SELF

Color variations based on a pattern of "call and recall" can also be observed in the work of Larry Potter. In his two untitled paintings of 1964 and 1965, the brushstrokes create patterns similar to musical riffs, organizing the space between background and surface. The lyrical abstract language that Potter developed in his late work, while he lived in Paris, is based on variations of the color planes. It is a language that tries to define the self and to establish an African-American cultural identity. Potter explains:

So it was with jazz that the Negro picks [sic] up the instruments from the immediate world around him and shaped a new music with personal rhythmic dreams driven by the collective dreams. Are they any possibility [sic] that these works shown here can have the stamp of my experience as a Negro?[12]

Potter lived abroad from 1956 until his death in 1966, a critical time of upheaval in the United States. His exile, also shared by other prominent African-American artists such as James Baldwin, may have influenced his questioning.

The search for self was a prominent theme in the art of the New York School, based in part on Surrealist techniques. This can be seen in Jackson Pollock's early paintings.[13] Pollock made a stylistic breakthrough in 1947 with his first drip-and-pour paintings. The technique incorporated elements of chance and accident, of performance and improvisation. The action of pouring paint can stand as a metaphor for the affirmation of self within a moment, a time sequence defined by the gesture. Such immediacy of action/perception implies an intimation of what constitutes the self. The importance of time sequences, the accelerated linear rhythms, and the repetition of patterns never exactly the same are shared with solo jazz improvisations. Such repetition/ variation of motifs can be observed in the two *Untitled* works [PLATES 12 AND 13] of 1950-51 in the exhibition.

Lee Krasner, in an often-quoted remark, confirmed the importance of jazz for Pollock:

[Jackson Pollock] would get into grooves of listening to his jazz records – not just for days – day and night, day and night for three days running, until you thought you would climb the roof!...Jazz? He thought it was the only other really creative thing happening in this country.[14]

The recording issued on the occasion of the recent Pollock retrospective at The Museum of Modern Art contains primarily big bands and early jazz; in addition, it has been established that Pollock liked sentimental songs as well as traditional jazz music.[15] Certainly, the fluidity and intuitive nature of Pollock's allover compositions and the rhythmic cadences of his drip-and-pour paintings are closely related to many forms of jazz. More specifically, his work of the late 1940s and early 1950s can be compared to bebop, with its rapidity of execution, staccato rhythms, and emphasis on linear variations. The lack of any one standpoint in the allover compositions and the heroic dimension of the early 1950s canvases are also comparable to Charlie Parker's succession of unlimited choruses.

Lee Krasner, who loved to dance to jazz music, sometimes allegedly with Mondrian,[16] considered improvisation a key to her creative process. Her collages are metaphors for reinventing the self, as well as for recycling, rewriting one's own history. In those of the 1950s and the 1980s, improvisation takes the form of a personal narrative.

It started in 1953 – I had the studio hung solidly with drawings, you know, floor to ceiling all around. Walked in one day, hated it all, took it down, tore everything and threw it on the floor, and when I went back – it was a couple of weeks before I opened that door again – it was seemingly a very destructive act. I don't know why I did it, except I certainly did it. When I opened the door and walked in, the floor was solidly covered with these torn drawings I had left and they began to interest me and I started collaging. Well, it started with drawings. Then I took my canvases and cut and began doing the same thing, and that ended in my collage show of 1955.[17]

The torn drawings were in part inspired by Pollock's large black-and-white drawings of 1951. By destroying them, Krasner was waging a war on the part of herself that had been influenced by Pollock and Mondrian.[18] Improvisation here is rooted in destruction as a ritual act from which new forms and new meaning emerge. *Burning Candles* [PLATE 9] of 1955 incorporates some of these torn fragments of drawings and canvases.

From the late 1970s into the 1980s, Krasner marked another pivotal point in her career with the use of collage. The materials were again old drawings, some of which she had done when she studied with Hans Hofmann between 1937 and 1940. The manner in which she applied sections of torn drawings to canvas can be seen in *Autumnal Red*. The subject here is the past and the need to look backward as well as go forward. Old works might not be relevant anymore, but they remain a source of creative renewal.

THE POLITICS OF IMPROVISATION

Norman Lewis was actively involved in the Civil Rights Movement.[19] From this engagement stems his specific place in post-war abstraction. He managed to close the gap between form and content, a divide that had been established by Modernism and exacerbated through the post-war years by Clement Greenberg and the formalist painters. Lewis interweaves formal and political content in paintings such as *Alabama*, a work inspired by the demonstration that followed the attempt by thirty-five African-American students to be served in the white-only cafeteria of the State Capitol on February 25, 1960. The cluster of figures around a luminous center symbolizes the political gathering, while the contrast between bright and dark stands as a metaphor for the racial and political tensions.

Lewis, who maintained a studio in Harlem during the 1950s, went regularly to the Apollo Theater and other nearby jazz clubs. Jazz was another important source for his visual system. *Playtime* [PLATE 10] evokes a jazz band by the color contrasts and angular shapes, much like the harmonies and rhythmic sequencing of the music. As Julian Euell noted:

Norman appreciated a wide range of literature, art and music. His library and record collection was substantial as well as impressive. His taste in music ran from blues to jazz to symphonies. He often played the blues on the piano for me. Although he listened to a wide range of music, his heart and soul were in the blues and the jazz.[20]

Lewis's paintings are characterized by flattened space, allover composition, and expressive brushwork – qualities shared by other post-war abstract artists, including Merton Simpson. Simpson combines expressionistic texture and allover composition in paintings such as *Universal Orchestration, Series A, 4A* [PLATE 17]. Simpson, himself a jazz musician, considers his own work a visual equivalent of music: "Musical improvisation and painting go hand in hand. Making a good painting is like playing a good solo."[21]

When Sam Gilliam started to drape canvas in 1968, he expanded his painting from the boundaries of the frame into open space: "It was free, it was untamed and they could be made in any length, without stretching, seventy-five feet to two hundred fifty yards."[22] The liberation of space in the draped canvases can be directly compared to the experimentation of free jazz in the 1960s. For Gilliam, improvisation relates to freedom of ideas and expression. In the political context of the late 1960s and early 1970s, his search is linked to the fight for justice and equality led by African Americans.

I particularly enjoyed the other day when Ornette Coleman said that what he does is great ideas. And I think that it sort of clears it up: it [improvisation] allows the ideas to be free, or to be different ideas.[23]

Gilliam structures the improvised stretching, folding, and hanging of canvas as he goes along, in response to the space in which he works. Such improvised structure is essential to these works, as well as to a series of collages of the mid-1970s inspired by the music of Miles Davis and John Coltrane. In fact, jazz has always been a source of inspiration for Gilliam:

I listened to jazz all my life. It was mostly jazz that accounted for the steps that I took as an abstract artist. In painting there was a need to go to what I call free steps. So, the precedence was there in Coltrane, Ornette Coleman. It was not that there was a map, but there was a possibility that existed because of those people.[24]

In the early 1990s, after a reassessment of his work, Gilliam began to concentrate on the effects of weight and gravity in relation to the entire structure. His draped site-specific canvases are architectural in the way they wrap space and reshape it. In the installation in this exhibition [PLATE 8], the visual rhythms generated by the draped materials and the color variations in the canvas transform the play of space as well as our perception of it.

Jazz was also a major creative force for Bob Thompson, who listened to music constantly in his Lower East Side studio. A regular patron of the Five Spot Cafe, Thompson heard performances by Eric Dolphy, Archie Shepp, and Ornette Coleman, with whom he became friends. In his work *Ornette* [PLATE 19] the simultaneous presentation of several viewpoints of the musician's face recalls Coleman's music, a complex form of non-linear improvisation that involved the playing of several instruments at once. When Coleman recorded his *Free Jazz* album in 1960, he joined two quartets for thirty-six minutes and twenty-three seconds in unrehearsed improvisation without harmonically structured design or even premeditated form.[25]

Thompson often appropriated from canonical works of Western art, a process that he related to the way jazz musicians constantly improvise upon and recreate old standards.[26] Thompson's improvisations included silhouetting, highly contrasted colors, and unconventional harmonies. Appropriation for him had nothing to do with political revisionism, reflecting instead his admiration for old European masters, notably those of the Renaissance. The multicolored people with whom he populates his paintings can be interpreted as a refusal of racial encoding. The vision that Thompson proposes seems closer to a form of multiracial and multicultural utopia than to a political protest. He was part of the downtown scene in the early 1960s, with its Beat poets, musicians, and painters, all of whom shared a belief in an ecumenical society.

Although Alma Thomas never claimed that her painting had any political dimensions, her rise to prominence reflected the political climate of these years. The context in which she was given a one-person exhibition at the Whitney Museum in 1972 is inscribed against a highly politicized background.[27] As a result of negotiations with the Black Emergency Cultural Coalition, the Whitney Museum committed to organizing five solo shows by African-American artists.[28] By doing so, the Whitney Museum could show its willingness to open its galleries to traditionally marginalized artists, while the absence of direct political content would make the exhibited works palatable to the conservative part of its constituency. Alma Thomas's was the last of these exhibitions.

Thomas drew her inspiration primarily from color and light effects in her garden. The composition of *Red Azaleas Singing and Dancing Rock and Roll Music* [PLATE 18] recalls multiple rhythmic and improvised musical sequences. Improvisation in Thomas's work consists of establishing surprise effects in an otherwise controlled structure. Like other late works, *Red Azaleas Singing and Dancing Rock and Roll Music* is composed around monochromatic variations that create allover orchestrations. Thomas completed the three panels, one at a time:

She often worked with one end of a large canvas in her lap while the rest of it was balanced against a sofa, absorbing the weight of the wooden canvas stretcher against her leg. Unable to back off in order to view her canvas from a distance, she simply kept turning the canvas to reach its unfinished areas.[29]

Watusi (Hard Edge), named after a 1960s dance song[30] and an African people, can be interpreted as a commentary on the way Africa was represented at the time. In *Watusi*, which resembles Matisse's 1953 collage *L'Escargot*, Thomas experimented with hard-edge painting, an approach favored by the Color Field artists with whom she became acquainted and associated. The rhythmic patterns and color variations in Thomas's work also bring to mind African-American quilts and relate to the tradition of "call and recall" reclaimed by Romare Bearden.

IMPROVISATION AS HISTORICAL NARRATIVE

Radcliffe Bailey chooses the elements in his mixed media works to create a narrative that recalls his personal history as well as that of the larger African-American community. Plow and axe handles, gourds, clay, shells, anvils, and copies of vintage photographs given to him by his grandmother are materials often encountered in his art. Bailey works in series, emphasizing the idea of variations upon a theme, a strategy shared by Davis, Bearden, Adkins, and Gilliam.

Mingus, Mingus [PLATE 3] is part of a series created in 1997, in which Bailey celebrates jazz musicians such as Rahsaan Roland Kirk, Duke Ellington, Billie Holiday, and the legendary bassist and composer Charles Mingus. Bailey improvises through associative meanings:

I think I improvise in several different ways. When I look at my work I see many different layers. For example I use the color blue that may reference indigo, and also the Blues, and evokes different moods, but I also see a religious meaning behind it, that relates to Yoruba and Dogon cultures.[31]

The reference to different African cultures is a common thread through his work. A single image is at the center of many of his constructions, recalling Nkisi BaKongo figures in which substances generating power are enshrined. In *Mingus, Mingus*, this position is occupied by an old photograph of a street band, a metaphor for past history. Historical references abound. On the surface of the bass-shaped work, one can see baseballs, which Bailey associates with jazz music. Although musicians and baseball players were celebrities, they faced segregation and racism throughout their careers. Axe handles and farming tools allude to the promise, made to freed slaves, of forty acres and a mule. White curvy patterns on the surface resemble Haitian *vévé* drawings used in *vaudou* ceremonies to announce or call deities, a status that Bailey bestows on jazz musicians of the caliber of Charles Mingus. Bailey creates a free form of storytelling by accumulating materials that suggest layers of meaning.

Ghanaian-born El Anatsui works in a similar accumulative fashion to evoke different aspects of African history. His pieces in the exhibition are composed of several discrete panels that are hung edge-to-edge. The wooden strips allow permutations and multiple combinations among the shapes, colors, and patterns of each work. The panels come from discarded timber, driftwood, recycled materials:

New wood requires the sculptor to reveal what's locked within, but with old wood, the action of time has worn away the prose, revealing the poetry of inner form.[32]

With a power saw, a chain saw, and a blowtorch, El Anatsui carved and burned the flat surfaces of the wood to create continuous networks of abstract patterns. The resulting designs resemble writing and in some recent works are inspired by Bamun scripts.[33] Other patterns are derived from the artist's knowledge of West African textiles. In *Grandma's Cloth IV* [PLATE 2] and *Wait make I commot my shirt* he combines Kente patterns from Ghana with those found in Akwete cloths from Nigeria, both places where the artist has lived. The use of a chain saw recalls other narratives:

That the chain saw expresses this radical increase in pace, and its excessive power, as it rips through soft wood, made me contemplate colonialism, the way the western powers carved up the African continent.[34]

El Anatsui's improvised visual system creates a language rich in layers of meaning that celebrate pre-colonial African history and insist upon aspects of a shared cultural memory.

IMPROVISATION AS TRANSCULTURAL STRATEGY

Terry Adkins, Ouattara, and Jean-Michel Basquiat approach their work from a transcultural perspective. Their paintings and sculptures are not framed by particular historical or cultural narratives; rather, they mix and match references to compose discourses that present a form of cultural synthesis.

A musician and performer himself, Terry Adkins created in 1997 a series of sculptures in homage to John Coltrane. Like most of Adkins's work since the late 1980s, these are made from scavenged materials that possess an inanimate presence because they contain memories of past lives and uses. The recycling process is analogous to the improvised treatment of standard songs in jazz, a process already evidenced in many works in the exhibition.

In the 1960s, Coltrane's music and thought incorporated Eastern religious beliefs, accenting the notions of union, indivisibility, and transcendence. The music became more spiritual in scope, aiming to embody a higher form of consciousness. The compositions lengthened into a continuous melodic flow played in an uninterrupted fashion, emulating the universal consciousness of divine nature. This transcendent aspect is echoed in Adkins's *Amen* [PLATE 1], which is shaped like a saxophone as well as a stairway. *Turyia* alludes to Alice Coltrane's spiritual name;[35] her involvement with Eastern spirituality is metaphorically rendered with suspended pearls. *Nenuphar*, the Persian word for the white water lily found in Europe,[36] may also refer to the lotus of Buddhist iconography. As a Persian symbol, it not only reflects Coltrane's influences, but also the importance of Moorish culture in the West. Adkins's piece is made of two truncated sousaphones[37] and alludes to the organic shape of the flower as well as to the ram's horns used in ancient liturgical music.[38] Such an accumulation of meanings creates an improvised discourse that reflects on culture as a composite ensemble.

Ouattara similarly synthesizes diverse sources in his work *Homage to Miles Davis* [PLATE 11]. Emphasizing the African ancestral origins of Davis and of jazz music in general, he gives Davis a royal Egyptian headdress; he collages the album cover onto a checkered background that recalls the spots of the leopard, a royal animal, as it appears in Nsibidi, an ancient initiatory writing of the Ejagham people of Nigeria, also found in the Americas. The "N:1" sign signals the position of Miles Davis at the pinnacle of World music. In this, as in other works, the encoding of information resembles the process by which cultures are formed and evolve, and here Ouattara places the accent upon the multidimensionality of jazz music and of American culture. In appropriating African motifs and patterns, integrating them into this monumental construction, and commingling ancient and contemporary histories, he shapes an open cultural space:

The spiritual school permits you to understand the world. You are allowed a vision that is cosmic rather than a nationalistic or village oriented one. Therefore you are the sun, the rain, the Mexican, the American, the Japanese, etc. It is the cosmic view of the world.[39]

In Ouattara's work, improvisation allows for the creation of a language born of the diverse cultures and societies in which he has lived and worked. Acknowledging the particularities of each source, it offers the freedom of inventing them afresh.

Basquiat listened to jazz as he worked and celebrated the music – particularly that of Charlie Parker and 1940s jazz – in several of his pieces; changes of tempo, breaks, and thematic variations are all characteristics of his visual language.

Basquiat activated an LP of free, Afro-Cuban and other kinds of jazz. Then he resumed work on an unfinished collage. Hard bop sounded. Jean Michel pasted on letters and crocodiles. He did this with a riffing insistence, matching the music…. Four styles of jazz – free, mambo inflected, hard bop and at the end fabulous early bop with sudden stops – accompanied the making of that collage.[40]

Basquiat's sensitivity to multiple rhythms and the breadth of his musical taste are echoed in his creative versatility and use of multiple images, materials, and modes of expression. His work channels a multitude of references from disparate sources: music, magazines, history books, museum catalogues. His early creations as the graffiti artist Samo were in fact improvised poetic writings. Indeed, pictograms, signs, and especially writing appear often in his work. In addition to jazz musicians, the Beat writers Jack Kerouac and William Burroughs were among his artistic role models.

Words and letters play an important role in the composition of *LNAPRK* [PLATE 4]. In other works, the juxtaposition of a crown and the acronym "CPRKR" alludes to Charlie Parker as a king; here we find a similar combination and play upon letters. The surface reads as an architectural structure covered with crossed-out words and repetitions of digits and musical notes, a system that emphasizes rhythms and improvisation. Pictograms of a house, a crown, and mask-like faces complete the imagery. The title suggests the old Coney Island amusement park, while the inscription "Italy in the 1500s" refers to one of Basquiat's heroes, Leonardo da Vinci. Such open-endedness and accumulation of images and meanings characterize Basquiat's creative process, as he constantly recombined his sources while systematically reinterpreting them.

The works by Basquiat, Adkins, and Ouattara transcend particular narratives, embracing multiple heroes, cultures, and values and echoing the breadth of jazz music itself. In their hands, improvisation creates languages that reflect a true sense of global culture.

The objects in this exhibition testify to the strength of improvisation as a visual process that incorporates multiple stories and historical accounts and transforms them into personal and social narratives. Historically, improvisation, with its power to change, has exemplified resilience and adaptation. As such, it has been used especially by immigrants to revise, reconstruct, and reshape their environment. As a creative process, it has allowed artists to reinvent themselves and their histories, opening the door to endless possibilities and constant renewal – always with serious playfulness.

ENDNOTES

1 Kandinsky titled some of his paintings "Improvisation" because he wanted to emulate the evocative power of music and its capacity to directly and powerfully translate emotions.

2 Irving Sandler: *The New York School* (New York: Harper & Row, 1978), p. 24.

3 Chad Mandeles, "Jackson Pollock and Jazz: Structural Parallels," *Arts Magazine*, vol. 56, no. 2 (October 1981), p. 139.

4 The seminal role played by jazz in the development of modern languages is also seen in the poetry and prose of the Beat Generation. Ginsberg, Ferlinghetti, Kerouac, Corso – all listened to jazz. The specific technique of "cut" that they developed in their poetry directly relates to the riffs and breaks of bebop and hard bop. Kerouac directly related his writing process to the way a jazz musician plays: "In the sense of a, say, tenor man drawing the breath and blowing a phrase on his saxophone, till he runs out of breath, and when he does, his sentence, his statement have been made...that's how therefore I separate my sentences, as breath separations of the mind....Then there's the raciness and freedom and humor of jazz instead of all that dreary analysis." (Irving Sandler, *The New York School*, p. 23).

5 John Lucas, "The Fine Art Jive of Stuart Davis," *Arts Magazine*, vol. 31, no. 10 (September 1957), p. 33.

6 Avis Berman, "Romare Bearden: 'I Paint Out of the Tradition of the Blues,'" *ARTnews*, vol. 79, no.10 (December 1980), p. 63.

7 Calvin Tomkins, "Putting Something Over Something Else," *The New Yorker*, November 28, 1977, p. 1.

8 John Lucas, "The Fine Art Jive of Stuart Davis," p. 33.

9 Frank Bowling, conversation with the author, July 2000.

10 Irving Sandler, *The New York School*, p. 108.

11 Avis Berman, "Romare Bearden: 'I Paint Out of the Tradition of the Blues,'" p. 60.

12 Diary of Larry Potter, unpublished materials, courtesy of June Kelly Gallery, New York.

13 Pollock was introduced to the surrealist idea of psychic automatism by Motherwell and Matta. With Krasner, Motherwell, and Baziotes, he experimented on several occasions with writing automatic poetry. The group also made automatic drawings and played the surrealist game of the *exquisite corpse*. For more information on the influence of Surrealism on Pollock's work, see David S. Rubin, "A Case for Content: Jackson Pollock's Subject Was the Automatic Gesture," *Arts Magazine*, vol. 53 (March 1979).

14 Chad Mandeles, "Jackson Pollock and Jazz: Structural Parallels," p. 139.

15 Helen Harrison, Director of the Pollock-Krasner House and Study Center, conversation with the author, July 2000.

16 Ibid.

17 Robert Hobbs, *Lee Krasner* (New York: Abbeville Press, 1993), p. 51.

18 Ibid., p. 51.

19 For more information on Norman Lewis's political role during the Civil Rights era, see David Craven, "Norman Lewis as Political Activist and Post Colonial Artist," *Norman Lewis Black Paintings, 1946-1977* (New York: The Studio Museum in Harlem, 1998).

20 Julian Euell, "Thoughts About Norman Lewis," *Norman Lewis: From the Harlem Renaissance to Abstraction* (New York: Kenkeleba Gallery, 1989), p. 52.

21 Angela D. Mack, *Merton D. Simpson: The Journey of an Artist* (Charleston: Gibbes Museum of Art, 1995), p. 14.

22 Sam Gilliam, conversation with the author, July 2000.

23 Ibid.

24 Ibid.

25 The album cover included a reproduction of Pollock's *White Light*, a painting of 1954. Coleman was not responsible for the choice of imagery.

26 Thelma Golden, *Bob Thompson* (New York: Whitney Museum of American Art, 1998), p. 19.

27 Activist organizations such as Art Workers Coalition, Women Artists in Revolution, and Black Emergency Cultural Coalition demonstrated and petitioned at the time against the traditional aesthetic standards of the museums. See Jonathan Binstock, "Apolitical Art in a Political World: Alma Thomas in the Late 1960s and Early 1970s," *Alma W. Thomas: A Retrospective of the Paintings* (Fort Wayne: Fort Wayne Museum of Art, 1998).

28 Jonathan Binstock, "Apolitical Art in a Political World," p. 64.

29 Romare Bearden and Harry Henderson, *A History of African-American Artists* (New York: Pantheon Books, 1993), p. 452.

30 *Watusi*, a song in which Africa was depicted from the quintessential colonialist and racist point of view, was recorded by Chubby Checker in 1961.

31 Radcliffe Bailey, conversation with the author, July 2000.

32 Gerard Houghton, "Ancestral Voices: El Anatsui," *World Sculpture News*, vol. 4, no. 2 (Spring 1998), p. 33.

33 Chika Okeke, "Slashing Wood, Eroding Culture: Conversation with El Anatsui," *Nka Journal of Contemporary African Art*, (8) (Spring 1997, Cornell University), p. 35.

34 Gerard Houghton, "Ancestral Voices: El Anatsui," p. 33.

35 Terry Adkins, conversation with the author, July 2000.

36 Ibid.

37 Nancy Princenthal, *Terry Adkins Later Coltrane* (New York: Emerson Gallery, Hamilton College, 1998), p. 17.

38 Ibid., p.17.

39 Thomas McEvilley, "An Interview with Ouattara," in *Fusion: West African Artists at The Venice Biennale* (New York: The Museum for African Art, 1993), p. 72.

40 Robert Farris Thompson, "Royalty, Heroism, and the Streets: The Art of Jean-Michel Basquiat," *Jean-Michel Basquiat* (New York: The Whitney Museum of American Art, 1993), p. 31.

BLUES FOR NOTE AND PAINT THERE HAS NEVER BEEN ANYTHING

more American than jazz. Jazz music remade every element of Western music in an American way, just as the Declaration of Independence and the Constitution remade the traditions of Western democracy, expanding the idea of freedom to levels it had never known at any prior time. American democracy updated the social order with its checks-and-balances system and its amendment process. These safeguard measures were based in tragic optimism, the idea that abuse of power can create tragic consequences but if there is a form in place that allows for the righting of wrongs, we can maintain an upbeat vision that is not naïve. When things assumed to be right turn out to be wrong, we have to improvise better policies into place. American democracy is an ongoing process that redefines itself through government in order to make up for the shortcomings of government. If the redefinition – as with the attempt at imposing temperance through law during the Prohibition era – doesn't work, we improvise ourselves out of a mess by striking a law from the books.

American democracy is also the governmental form in which the interplay between the individual and the mass takes on a complexity mirrored by the improvising unit of the jazz band. In jazz music, the empathetic imagination of the individual strengthens the ensemble. This happens as the form, which is an outline that is followed but is also played with, is given its dimensions through the collective inventions of the ensemble. In that sense, jazz is a democratic form itself, one in which, as the great jazz critic Martin Williams observed, there is more freedom than ever existed in any previous Western music.

That freedom affected everything that jazz touched. The instruments were played with such redefining conceptions that one could even say that the tools of the music were aesthetically remade. For vocal effects, jazz musicians held rubber plungers in front of the bells of trumpets and trombones, moving them so that the human voice with an American accent marinated in the blues whispered or surged into the air. Reed instruments became vocal as well as string-like and percussive. The string bass, almost always bowed in European concert music, was plucked into an unprecedented kind of heavy-stringed, harmonic percussion. Drums and cymbals were brought together and resulted in an entirely new instrument called the drum set, one which called upon the player's hands and feet. The piano may have been the most resistant but it, too, submitted to a jazz identity, loping through and trilling the blues and swinging with yet another vista of tuned percussion at the ready. At the will of Thelonious Monk, the piano became something truly new, a harshly lyrical reflection of the steel and concrete form of New York City.

The instruments were changed because they had to express another sensibility, and that sensibility was given its force through the blues, the show tunes, and the original works that formed the basic repertoire of the music. That music was rough at one end and quite refined at the other, arriving from a Negro world of black, brown, beige, and bone-colored people. These were the descendants of slaves and the heirs to bloodlines and layers of culture so profound one can easily understand how jazz rose from those wild to graceful circumstances and was passed on for all to share by the Negro, whom Richard Wright thought of as America's metaphor, the symbol of the best and the most difficult aspects of this nation. Like the people who invented it, jazz came up hard, rising from the blues and out of the gutbuckets where the stickiness and the stink of life as well as its sensual truths and its delicious but slippery textures were evident.

Though it is often resisted and resented, the fact is that the music arrived in New Orleans, that port city where one could hear chants in the streets, blues, funeral marches, parade music, and, in the elegant theaters, the French and Italian opera. A musician coming to maturity in the Crescent City played christenings, weddings, funerals, Mardi Gras, park concerts, and just about anything there was to play, discovering the wide range of human occasions that demanded appropriate rhythms and tunes. Jazz was a development of that amalgamation, an art built upon one talent after another, some trained, some not – which is why the music grew so fast; it was open to anyone who could make musical sense. If the musician could perform with logic, feeling, and command of the idiom, it didn't matter if the voice had a small range or the instrumentalist wasn't effective in more than one register. There was a place for that musician and that musician, like Billie Holiday, might powerfully influence jazz interpretation. So the music, part quilt and available to any kind of true talent, achieved originality in the same way that all things do; it became more than the parts forming it.

What held those parts together was itself original, an American feeling that arrived around the turn of the twentieth century. They called it the blues. The blues was the tragic and optimistic thread that wove together the various kinds of musical fabrics, from tattered sandpaper underwear to the highest quality silk. It was through blues melody, blues feeling, and blues rhythm that an adult American music arose. In the name of blues, a simple form full of profound feeling came into being, one in which the listener was taken beyond sentimentality into a fluctuating world of deep heartache and lust and frustration and exaltation and rage and remorse and the voluminous memories of tenderness triumphant through the fury against loneliness that is the rhythm of love and romance.

The rhythm of swing, which was brought to an innovative level of phrasing by Louis Armstrong during the middle and late twenties, gave jazz the rhythmic distinction that matched the melodic originality and the harmonic freshness of blues. With his melodic invention, his swing, and the way in which he was able to push the blues through the harmonies of the Tin Pan Alley tunes that provided a bridge from the world of jazz into the broader society, Armstrong became one of the great creators of the twentieth century. From his range of improvised ideas comes the core of jazz, the roots upon which all the soloists, the rhythm section players, and the composers built their music, consciously or not. That combination of familiar and unfamiliar themes artistically realized through improvised development provided another flying machine for the human soul.

Just as improvisation is central to jazz, it is improvisation that has long defined so many kinds of visual art as well. Jazz and Western visual art have much more in common than we usually think, and that is why any gallery show featuring jazz works has the potential to highlight that commonality while making us even more aware of how superbly different the silent work of the visual artist is from the aural art of the musician. The essence of those differences arrives through the materials used to create the aesthetic work. When the subjects are painting and music, we are talking about images or sound achieving communication with the eyes or the ears of the audience. It is through those two very different senses that the sensibility of the audience is touched, sometimes on many, many levels. That is why we can think of the unspeaking art of the painter as the art of the visible, and the audible but unseeable art of the musician as the art of the invisible.

It is impossible to say which one – music or painting – arrived first. But I mean as an art, not just a pleasurable activity. During the childish years of the species, way back before way back, there were surely people who made noise. They were most probably having fun; expression in precise terms or in poetic abstractions were not at the top of the list of ambitions. There were just as surely people who scratched upon something or, even earlier, stood amused at the fact that they could make impressions with their feet or their hands – or both – in the dirt or in the mud. The evolution into art is something else altogether because the aesthetic proposes that symbols can magnetize worlds of experience and propel them into an audience at the same time. In both visual art and music, that is the problem facing the artist – how well can something summon and how well can it project.

The means through which the vision of the artist is made manifest help determine what is at work, and those means are so often improvisational or are approached with improvisational freedom. There are certain elements that arrive over and over in jazz and they have their parallels in visual art. In jazz, even in its period of most substantial innovation, the music far more often than not uses 4/4 swing, fast, medium, and slow. Romantic and contemplative ballads are played. The blues is fundamental to the music. And there are uses of Afro-Hispanic rhythms, sometimes called "Latin." In painting, there is the portrait, there is the landscape, there is the still life, there is the religious work, and so on and on. Where jazz and painting really seem related is in the fact that the maker may often take something that is common and, through the improvisations native to bringing forth individuality, restate the very proposition.

Some examples are perhaps necessary. In the world of the painter as in the world of the jazz musician, there is a standard repertoire, a body of themes that have become quite familiar to the audience. The Italian Renaissance is a case in point. The themes were so often biblical and focused on the life of Christ that those themes rendered by the individual artist were dominated by improvisation. The painter got a chance to choose everything once he had decided upon his theme. From the annunciation to the crucifixion, the miracles to the descent from the cross, the lamentations to the ascension, there was an open sky of decisions that constituted improvisation. The painter could decide what time of day it was and, therefore, what position the sun would be in, determining the point of light and the quality of the shadows and the darkness. The painter could decide what was in the foreground and what was in the background. The facial features and the positions of the figures were equally open to improvisation as were the colors of the clothes and the surrounding combination of landscape and human elements of construction (including the texture of the wood of the cross).

So painters have a good deal in common with jazz musicians, regardless of when they arrived after painting had revealed its powers through perspective. From that point on, we were moving toward the kind of work we see in this show, work that attempts to bring to the canvas, in a silent way, the improvised human song that we hear on jazz bandstands. Jazz musicians, speaking of formal control and substance, have often talked of a first class improviser as one who "paints a picture." In this show, ample evidence is presented of how improvisation functions in the quiet world of the visual image. We see the human form toyed with, flat rejections of perspective, collages, totally abstract works that attempt to put painting into the abstract arena of feeling and nuance that is the province of the musician. In all, we see many approaches, all of them the expression of freedom, all of them in the spirit of jazz, which is in the spirit of the United States of America.

Jazz AND VISUAL IMPROVISATIONS

PLATE 1   20

terry adkins AMEN 1998, STEEL, POLYCHROME WOOD, 115 × 17 × 54, COLLECTION OF THE ARTIST

PLATE 2   21

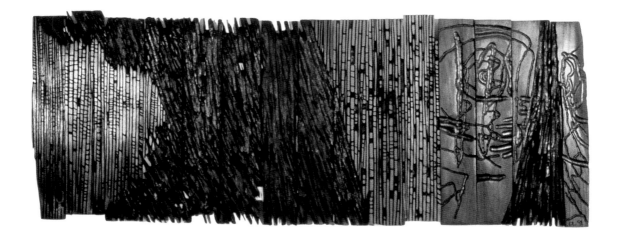

eL anaTSUI GRANDMA'S CLOTH IV 1991, AFRICAN HARDWOOD, 23 × 61, COURTESY SKOTO GALLERY, NEW YORK, NY

PLATE 3   22

RaDCLiffe BaiLeY MINGUS, MINGUS 1997, MIXED MEDIA ON WOOD, 109 × 48 × 9½, A.B. RICHMAN

PLATE 4   23

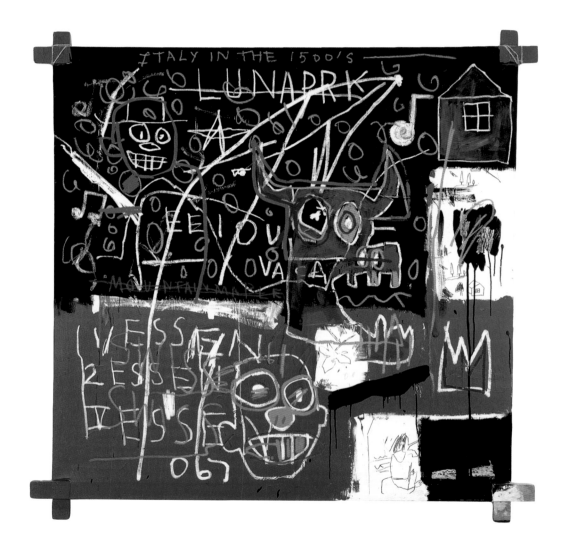

Jean-Michel Basquiat LNAPRK 1982, SYNTHETIC POLYMER AND OIL STICK ON CANVAS, 73 1/2 × 72 1/4, WHITNEY MUSEUM OF AMERICAN ART, NEW YORK, GIFT OF JUNE AND PAUL SCHORR IN HONOR OF THE 60TH ANNIVERSARY OF THE WHITNEY MUSEUM OF AMERICAN ART, © 2001 ARTISTS RIGHTS SOCIETY (ARS), NEW YORK/ADAGP, PARIS

PLATE 5   24

romare bearden IMPROVISATIONS 1969, COLLAGE ON BOARD, 10¼ × 13, SHELDON ROSS

PLATE 6   25

FRANK BOWLING ORNETTESCORNET 1994, OIL AND ACRYLIC ON CANVAS, 32 × 20, RUPERT A. THOMPSON, M.D.

PLATE 7 26

STUART DAVIS PAD NO. 4 1947, OIL ON CANVAS, 14 × 18, LENT BY BROOKLYN MUSEUM OF ART, BEQUEST OF EDITH AND MILTON LOWENTHAL, 1992.11.5

PLATE 8   27

sam gilliam BIKERS AND SWALLOWS 2000, MIXED MEDIA, PAINTED AND COLLAGED SURFACES WITH ALUMINUM FOILS AND PIANO HINGES, 120 × 144, SITE-SPECIFIC INSTALLATION BY THE ARTIST

PLATE 9   28

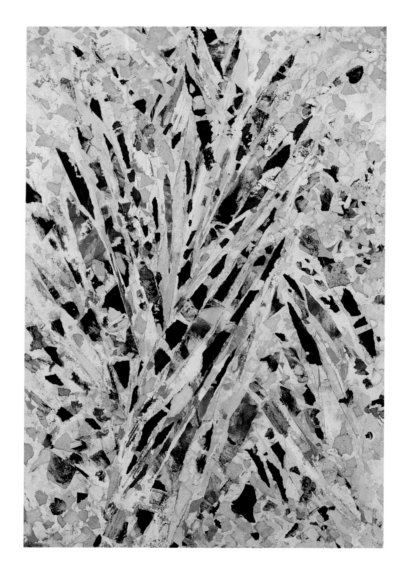

Lee Krasner **BURNING CANDLES** 1955, OIL, PAPER, AND CANVAS ON LINEN, 58 × 39, COLLECTION NEUBERGER MUSEUM OF ART, PURCHASE COLLEGE, STATE UNIVERSITY OF NEW YORK, GIFT OF ROY R. NEUBERGER

PLATE 10

29

norman lewis PLAYTIME 1966, OIL ON CANVAS, 44³/₄ × 77, THE ESTATE OF NORMAN W. LEWIS

PLATE 11   30

ouattara HOMAGE TO MILES DAVIS 1996, MIXED MEDIA ON CANVAS, 88 × 61½, COLLECTION OF ANDRE HARRELL, NEW YORK

Jackson Pollock UNTITLED C. 1950-51 (CATALOGUE RAISONNÉ #38), SILKSCREEN, BLACK INK ON RED PAPER, 8³/₈ × 5, COURTESY JOAN T. WASHBURN GALLERY, NEW YORK AND THE POLLOCK-KRASNER FOUNDATION, INC.

Jackson Pollock UNTITLED C. 1950-51 (CATALOGUE RAISONNÉ #39), SILKSCREEN, YELLOW INK ON RED PAPER, 8¹/₂ × 5¹/₂, COURTESY JOAN T. WASHBURN GALLERY, NEW YORK AND THE POLLOCK-KRASNER FOUNDATION, INC.

PLATE 14

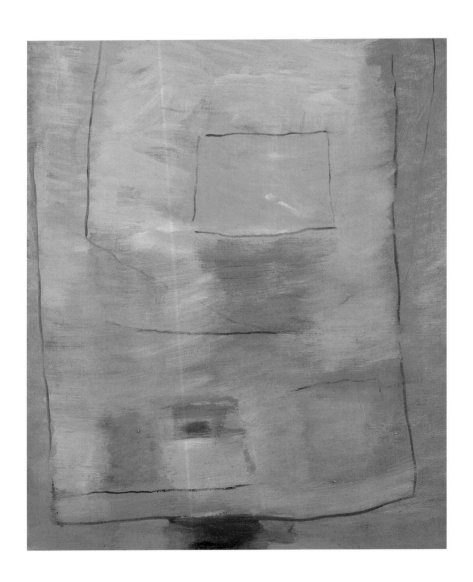

LARRY POTTER UNTITLED 1965, OIL ON LINEN, 31³/₄ × 25¹/₂, COLLECTION OF CHERYL L. SUTTON, COURTESY JUNE KELLY GALLERY, NEW YORK

PLATE 15   33

LARRY RIVERS **THE DRUMMER** 1958, OIL ON CANVAS, 68 × 58, ON LOAN FROM THE COLLECTION OF CLAUDIA, KATHRYN, AND PATRICIA WEILL

PLATE 16

34

CHARLES SELIGER NEARER THE STARS 1995, ACRYLIC ON MASONITE, 14 × 14, COURTESY OF MICHAEL ROSENFELD GALLERY, NEW YORK, NY

PLATE 17　　　　　　　　　　　　　35

merton simpson UNIVERSAL ORCHESTRATION, SERIES A, 4A 1983, OIL AND ACRYLIC ON BOARD, 18 × 24, MERTON D. SIMPSON

PLATE 18   36

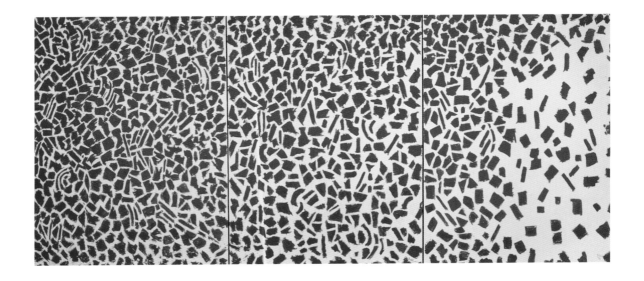

alma Thomas RED AZALEAS SINGING AND DANCING ROCK AND ROLL MUSIC 1976, ACRYLIC ON CANVAS, 72¼ × 156¾,
SMITHSONIAN AMERICAN ART MUSEUM, BEQUEST OF THE ARTIST

PLATE 19   37

BOB THOMPSON ORNETTE 1960-61, OIL ON CANVAS, 81 × 77³/₁₆, COLLECTION OF DAVID ANDERSON

CHECKLIST DIMENSIONS ARE IN INCHES HEIGHT × WIDTH × DEPTH

TERRY ADKINS

AMEN 1998, STEEL, POLYCHROME WOOD, 115 × 17 × 54, COLLECTION OF THE ARTIST
NENUPHAR 1998, BRASS, COPPER, 29 × 69 × 9, COLLECTION OF THE ARTIST
SILVER SONIC 1995, BRASS, 4 HORNS, 216 × 24 × 24 EACH, COLLECTION OF THE ARTIST
TURIYA 1998, BARITONE SAXOPHONE CASE WITH MIXED MEDIA, 19 × 44 × 16, COLLECTION OF THE ARTIST

EL ANATSUI

GRANDMA'S CLOTH IV 1991, AFRICAN HARDWOOD, 23 × 61, COURTESY SKOTO GALLERY, NEW YORK, NY
WAIT MAKE I COMMOT MY SHIRT 1993, AFRICAN HARDWOOD, 44 × 24, COURTESY SKOTO GALLERY, NEW YORK, NY

RADCLIFFE BAILEY

MINGUS, MINGUS 1997, MIXED MEDIA ON WOOD, 109 × 48 × 9$\frac{1}{2}$, A.B. RICHMAN

JEAN-MICHEL BASQUIAT

LNAPRK 1982, SYNTHETIC POLYMER AND OIL STICK ON CANVAS, 73$\frac{1}{2}$ × 72$\frac{1}{4}$, WHITNEY MUSEUM OF AMERICAN ART, NEW YORK ,
GIFT OF JUNE AND PAUL SCHORR IN HONOR OF THE 60TH ANNIVERSARY OF THE WHITNEY MUSEUM OF AMERICAN ART

ROMARE BEARDEN

IMPROVISATIONS 1969, COLLAGE ON BOARD, 10$\frac{1}{4}$ × 13, SHELDON ROSS
SOUL THREE 1968, COLLAGE ON BOARD, 44 × 55$\frac{1}{2}$, COURTESY OF MICHAEL ROSENFELD GALLERY, NEW YORK, NY
UPTOWN SUNDAY NIGHT SESSION 1981, MIXED MEDIA, PAPER COLLAGE ON BOARD, 44 × 56, COLLECTION OF GEORGE AND JOYCE WEIN

FRANK BOWLING

ABOUTMIDNIGHTLASTNIGHT 1982, OIL AND ACRYLIC ON CANVAS, 97 × 71, COLLECTION OF THE ARTIST
ORNETTESCORNET 1994, OIL AND ACRYLIC ON CANVAS, 32 × 20, RUPERT A. THOMPSON, M.D.

STUART DAVIS

PAD NO. 4 1947, OIL ON CANVAS, 14 × 18, LENT BY BROOKLYN MUSEUM OF ART, BEQUEST OF EDITH AND MILTON LOWENTHAL, 1992.11.5
UNTITLED 1947, GOUACHE, 9 × 11, COLLECTION OF EARL DAVIS, COURTESY SALANDER-O'REILLY GALLERIES, NYC

SAM GILLIAM

BIKERS AND SWALLOWS 2000, MIXED MEDIA, PAINTED AND COLLAGED SURFACES WITH ALUMINUM FOILS AND PIANO HINGES, 120 × 144,
SITE-SPECIFIC INSTALLATION BY THE ARTIST

LEE KRASNER

AUTUMNAL RED 1980, OIL AND COLLAGE ON CANVAS, 55$\frac{3}{4}$ × 73, © POLLOCK-KRASNER FOUNDATION, INC., COURTESY ROBERT MILLER GALLERY, NY
BURNING CANDLES 1955, OIL, PAPER, AND CANVAS ON LINEN, 58 × 39, COLLECTION NEUBERGER MUSEUM OF ART, PURCHASE COLLEGE,
STATE UNIVERSITY OF NEW YORK, GIFT OF ROY R. NEUBERGER

norman Lewis
ALABAMA 1960, OIL ON CANVAS, 48 × 72¼, THE ESTATE OF NORMAN W. LEWIS
FROLIC 1971, OIL ON CANVAS, 50¾ × 70½, COURTESY BILL HODGES GALLERY, NEW YORK
PLAYTIME 1966, OIL ON CANVAS, 44¾ × 77, THE ESTATE OF NORMAN W. LEWIS

ouattara
HOMAGE TO MILES DAVIS 1996, MIXED MEDIA ON CANVAS, 88 × 61½, COLLECTION OF ANDRE HARRELL, NEW YORK

Jackson POLLOCK
UNTITLED C. 1950-51 (CATALOGUE RAISONNÉ #38), SILKSCREEN, BLACK INK ON RED PAPER, 8⅜ × 5, COURTESY JOAN T. WASHBURN GALLERY, NEW YORK AND THE POLLOCK-KRASNER FOUNDATION, INC.
UNTITLED C. 1950-51 (CATALOGUE RAISONNÉ #39), SILKSCREEN, YELLOW INK ON RED PAPER, 8½ × 5½, COURTESY JOAN T. WASHBURN GALLERY, NEW YORK AND THE POLLOCK-KRASNER FOUNDATION, INC.
UNTITLED C. 1950-51 (CATALOGUE RAISONNÉ #42), SILKSCREEN, BLACK INK ON WHITE PAPER, 8½ × 5½, COURTESY JOAN T. WASHBURN GALLERY, NEW YORK AND THE POLLOCK-KRASNER FOUNDATION, INC.

Larry POTTER
UNTITLED 1964, OIL ON LINEN, 38½ × 31¼, COURTESY JUNE KELLY GALLERY, NEW YORK
UNTITLED 1965, OIL ON LINEN, 31¾ × 25½, COLLECTION OF CHERYL L. SUTTON, COURTESY JUNE KELLY GALLERY, NEW YORK

Larry RIVERS
THE DRUMMER 1958, OIL ON CANVAS, 68 × 58, ON LOAN FROM THE COLLECTION OF CLAUDIA, KATHRYN, AND PATRICIA WEILL

Charles Seliger
LEGEND 1993, ACRYLIC ON MASONITE, 11 × 14¾, COURTESY OF MICHAEL ROSENFELD GALLERY, NEW YORK, NY
NEARER THE STARS 1995, ACRYLIC ON MASONITE, 14 × 14, COURTESY OF MICHAEL ROSENFELD GALLERY, NEW YORK, NY

merton Simpson
POLYTONICS 3 1983-84, OIL AND ACRYLIC ON BOARD, 35 × 52, MERTON D. SIMPSON
UNIVERSAL ORCHESTRATION, SERIES A, 4A 1983, OIL AND ACRYLIC ON BOARD, 18 × 24, MERTON D. SIMPSON

alma Thomas
RED AZALEAS SINGING AND DANCING ROCK AND ROLL MUSIC 1976, ACRYLIC ON CANVAS, 72¼ × 156¾, SMITHSONIAN AMERICAN ART MUSEUM, BEQUEST OF THE ARTIST
WATUSI (HARD EDGE) 1963, ACRYLIC ON CANVAS, 47⅝ × 44¼, HIRSHHORN MUSEUM AND SCULPTURE GARDEN, SMITHSONIAN INSTITUTION, GIFT OF VINCENT MELZAC, ARLINGTON, VIRGINIA, 1976

BOB Thompson
ORNETTE 1960-61, OIL ON CANVAS, 81 × 77³/₁₆, COLLECTION OF DAVID ANDERSON
UNTITLED 1963, OIL ON CANVAS, 63 × 86½, COURTESY OF MICHAEL ROSENFELD GALLERY, NEW YORK, NY

PHOTO CREDITS
PHOTOGRAPHS OF THE WORKS OF ART IN THIS EXHIBITION
HAVE BEEN SUPPLIED BY THE OWNERS OR CUSTODIANS OF
THE WORKS, AS CITED IN THE CAPTIONS. THE FOLLOWING
LIST APPLIES TO PHOTOGRAPHS FOR WHICH AN ADDITIONAL
ACKNOWLEDGMENT IS DUE.

EL ANATSUI, GRANDMA'S CLOTH IV, 1991
SPENCER RICHARDS
LEE KRASNER, BURNING CANDLES, 1955
JIM FRANK
OUATTARA, HOMAGE TO MILES DAVIS, 1996
ROBERT MCKEEVER
ALMA THOMAS, WATUSI (HARD EDGE), 1963
LEE STALSWORTH
BOB THOMPSON, ORNETTE, 1960-61
ELIZABETH DAVIS